Choose MY Happy Place

A short cut to a happier next stage in life.

Rose Thun

Choose MY Happy Place © Copyright <<2021>> Rose Thun

For more information, email hello@choosemyhappyplace.com.

ISBN: 978-0-578-31199-9

GET THE COMPANION PRIORITIES WORKBOOK FREE!

To get the best experience with this book, you'll want to download and use the Choose MY Happy Place Priorities Workbook so you are able to implement faster and take the next steps needed to reach your happy place sooner.

While you're there, if you are feeling like you just want to see information about lots of US places, and not dive into your priorities yet, then download the **Free Reports Bundle**.

Download your FREE copy of each by scanning the QR code or visiting:

https://www.choosemyhappyplace.com/choose-my-happy-place-report-bundle

Dedication

Dedicated to you, the reader, for making your life better.

Contents

Notes to the Reader

I realize some readers like to skip between sections as they read, so a few notes about that process. The steps build upon each other. You should identify your why before you do the subsequent steps; but there is more flexibility in the sequence of later exercises.

Quotes are highlighted.

Prompts and exercises for the reader are put into table formats.

Prompt or exercise	Additional considerations	Additional considerations
Space for your answers	Space for your answers	Space for your answers

OR

Prompt or exercise
Space for your answers

To get the best experience with this book, I recommend you download and use the Choose MY Happy Place Priorities Workbook so you are able to implement faster and take the next steps needed to reach your happy place sooner.

It may also be helpful to take the **Choose MY Happy Place What Mistakes May Keep You From Thriving Quiz.**
choosemyhappyplace.com/**quiz**

Introduction

If you're feeling itchy for a change, burned out, or are in analysis paralysis about what's next, **Choose MY Happy Place** is a short cut to get you to your better next stage of life quicker.

This book is an introduction to the curated data of what makes people happy, with tools to help identify what makes you happy quickly. We'll address fears, clarify what's essential, and <u>see</u> what may be keeping you from thriving.

You might find you want to move, or that you don't, or discover it's something else entirely that needs to change for you to be happier. This book will help you design a better life, no matter where you choose to live.

By the end of this book, you will be holding your priorities short list in your hands. That priorities short list is the platform to launch a life optimized for you, and you can do this in a weekend.

Take the shortcut to your happy place.

1- WHY?

My Whys

My own experiences deciding where and how to live, and my surveys of thousands of people, point to some common themes that led to this book.

1. **My own happier life!** I have burned out, switched careers, landscapes, industries, downshifted, worked like a maniac, and experimented with life hacks and lifestyles for decades. I'm too young to retire and too old to put up with a miserable grind. This book is a nice way to distill some essentials and write a happier story for my own life. These are the tools I come back to.

   As Brianna Wiest so eloquently observed in ***101 Essays That Will Change The Way You Think***, the gap between realization and taking action is filled with needless suffering; which I'd prefer to avoid.

Adapted from Brianna Wiest's *101 Essays That Will Change the Way You Think*

2. **Other people seem unhappy too.** I am hearing my friends and people who read my newsletter feeling stuck; in analysis paralysis, burned out, uncertain, overthinking, overcomplicating and wallowing. This book has tools to help; it is a short cut process to map what makes you happy so you can start creating a better future.

This idea of Choose MY Happy Place actually started on a lark because of my friends. My friend D was trying to decide where to retire and said she could pick more features for an engagement ring than on where to retire. It seemed absurd. But she was right.

My friend B retired to FL - thrilled at the idea of sunshine, beaches, family and a great new house. She immediately regretted it. There's no Trader Joes she lamented....and the yoga studios are awful. And then she awoke to an alligator nose to nose with her dog through the screen of her lanai. That did it. She's moved back to Maryland and then went back to work; missing her tribe and sense of purpose.

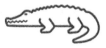

I have so many friends feeling like they are ready for a change but not sure where to go next. The conversations got my curiosity going, and the deep dive into the data began... after many months of collecting and analyzing, I've gleaned some surprising results and wonderful reports and tools that I'm sharing so you can stop feeling stuck and start finding what works well for you.

And after many months I've also learned most people don't really move and often don't enjoy retirement. And moving is not the first issue to decide. Getting clarity on your priorities is a prerequisite to being happy, wherever you live.

I have also noticed a comical surge in the number of middle age men biking on the roads near my house. While I am over my own I-must-do-a-marathon streak, I fully empathize about their striving. Apparently, it is a new way to do midlife crisis.

While we hardly talk about midlife crises anymore, people tend to muddle through quietly, individually. It's a term I think of as applying to my parents' generation, not mine, but the trends suggest we just do them differently.

> **"Welcome to the modern - and mindful - midlife crisis, where you're more likely to run a marathon than run away from your marriage. It's less splurging on a Porsche, more searching for your purpose. As for trading in your spouse for a younger model? So last decade. Today's crisis involves swapping your corporate career for something more meaningful."[1]**

3. **The 2019 World Happiness Report[2] is one of the most depressing things I've read in ages.** When I read "In most countries, as wealth increases, happiness increases…only the United States is one of the richest countries in the world and also one of the most unhappy and addicted societies." I was astounded to see how widespread this is. I want to help more people choose their happy places and to thrive.

4. **So many people don't know what's important to happiness:** The surprising data on what makes people happy tells us that it's not all about the money. Yes, you

---

[1] https://www.smh.com.au/lifestyle/life-and-relationships/midlife-crisis-gen-x-style-less-running-away-more-running-marathons-20200626-p556h6.html
[2] Helliwell, J., Layard, R., & Sachs, J. (2019). World Happiness Report 2019, New York: Sustainable Development Solutions Network.

need to have your basic needs met, and more money does make people happier, but money is not a prerequisite for happiness. So many people don't seem to know this fact.

5. **Happiness is pivotal to so much more**
   My background is in consulting - to improve teams and product development. The happiness of a team and sense of purpose are the fundamental bedrock for success; in whatever way you choose to define success. Gallup polls have proven it. With this book, I've shifted my focus to the personal, because what could be more important to get right than your own life? It's a starting point for everything else. As Erik Barker, author of *Barking Up the Wrong Tree: The Surprising Science Behind Why Everything You Know About Success Is (Mostly) Wrong* so eloquently says:

   > **"If we can get somebody to raise their levels of optimism or deepen their social connection or raise happiness, turns out every single business and educational outcome we know how to test for improves dramatically. You can increase your success rates for the rest of your life and your happiness levels will flatline, but if you raise your level of happiness and deepen optimism it turns out every single one of your success rates rises dramatically compared to what it would have been at negative, neutral, or stressed."[3]**

   ## *Who can refuse increasing every single success criterion dramatically?*

   ## *Not me.*

---

[3] https://www.bakadesuyo.com/2014/09/be-more-successful/

Your Why

"Start with Why"

-Simon Sinek

More important than my whys, are yours. This is the foundation you need to start with on your path to getting to your happy place. If you're not clear about why you want to make a change, it's quite easy to procrastinate, lose sight of it, get caught up in the day to day…and not get there! What catalyzed you to pick up this book?

Are you burned out, feeling stuck, retirement isn't what you expected, have a health issue, a recent breakup, pandemic malaise, or just a restlessness that there must be something more, list out all the reasons you want to change your life.

Your Why

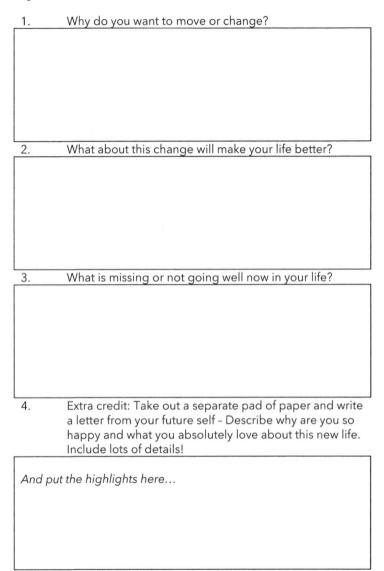

1. Why do you want to move or change?

2. What about this change will make your life better?

3. What is missing or not going well now in your life?

4. Extra credit: Take out a separate pad of paper and write a letter from your future self - Describe why are you so happy and what you absolutely love about this new life. Include lots of details!

And put the highlights here...

Use this foundation you need to start with on your path to getting to your happy place. You may want to come back when you're tempted to stop or when you need an arbiter in your decisions.

If you're hesitant to write in this book, don't be. Play tick tack toe, scribble like a 3 year old, make a doodle, just get over that resistance in the space below and then go back and fill in your Why.

If you really can't write in this book, go download and print the free companion Choose MY Happy Place Priorities Workbook to fill in.

Choose MY Happy Place What Mistakes May Keep You From Thriving Quiz.

You may want to take the quiz to see where you tend to focus in thinking about how to the future and the free report that details some of the risks and what you might be missing.

choosemyhappyplace.com/**quiz**

The 4 main areas where people focus are summarized below.

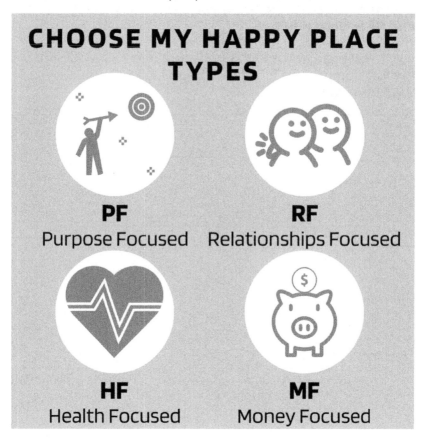

The Choose MY Happy Place Blueprint

With your WHY defined, you're off to a good start. Let's keep the momentum going with the Blueprint Path to My Happy Place!

CHOOSE MY HAPPY PLACE BLUEPRINT

Why do I want a change?

What fears or beliefs limit my thinking?

What makes people happy in general?

What makes me happy specifically?

What is my priorities short list?

What is my plan and next steps to take?

Are the new changes working well; how to improve?

Now you're on the road to your happy place. Let's go over a few sticking points that often occur next.

2- Getting Unstuck

"By taking the safest path possible many people end up living a life they'd never consciously have chosen.[4]"

-Margie Warrell

Inaction breeds doubt and fear. Action breeds confidence and courage.

-Dale Carnegie

"Time is short, my strength is limited, the office is a horror, the apartment is noisy, and if a pleasant, straightforward life is not possible, then one must try to wriggle through by subtle maneuvers."
-Franz Kafka

What fears or beliefs limit your thinking and life and how do you mitigate them?

To avoid regrets and live life to the fullest, we may have to take Kafka's advice for subtle maneuvers to get the action started.

Feeling stuck and the inaction that follows emerges from fear, concerns and uncertainty. It leaks out in many ways: procrastination, resistance, indecision, disagreements that seem unresolvable, and the one I wallow in most often, over complicating. I always have the sense that if I just read one more book or paper, it will give me the answer I am seeking, … and I can read for a long time.

---

[4] https://www.forbes.com/sites/margiewarrell/2013/03/19/the-parmenides-fallacy-are-you-ignoring-the-cost-of-inaction/?sh=1615dc5166e8

Not deciding is a decision though. Inaction is both a cause and a symptom of fear. Lingering in it will make you unhappy. Recent research showed that **"people feel the most intense regret in relation to regretted actions or inactions that they have an ongoing (but untaken) opportunity to correct"**. **The research also says lifetime regret of inactions is more frequent than of actions.** [5]

If you don't address your fears (concerns, questions, limiting beliefs, excuses, whatever you prefer to call them), you'll likely stay mired in inaction. I consider it the next step in the foundation of the path to your happy place. There are a few powerful ways to deal with fear. The first, stoic fear setting, feels analytical to me; and is wonderful for technical and financial decisions and fears. The second, "how interesting" provides the space for the third tool. The third tool, reframing, works really well for self-limiting beliefs, doubts and fears. I often use them together.

Stoic Fear Setting

The first way to address your fears, concerns, or resistance is with Fear Setting. It's an ancient idea with a modern introduction from author and podcaster Tim Ferriss. He describes it in a YouTube video *Why you should define your fears instead of your goals* | Tim Ferriss [6] where he espouses this stoic practice he does quarterly. Specifically, he recommends:

1. Separate what you can control from what you cannot, then focus on what you can control and act on.
2. Define your fear and the worst possible outcome.
3. Define how you can prevent those fears from happening
4. Identify how you could mitigate the worst-case outcomes if they do happen.
5. Think about what your life will look like if you don't take action for 6 months, 12 months, or 3 years and then

[5] Front. Psychol., 15 December 2016 | https://doi.org/10.3389/fpsyg.2016.01941
[6] https://www.youtube.com/watch?app=desktop&v=5J6jAC6XxAl

compare the choice of doing to do the fearful thing instead inaction.

In my experience, this is an iterative process but every iteration leads you to reach a better state and choose a more helpful way to act.

My Fear	What is the worst possible outcome of my fear?	How to prevent that worst possible outcome of my fear?	How to repair that worst possible outcome of my fear if it does happen?	What will my life look like if I don't take action
e.g. I am going to be living in a van down by the river	I actually do end up in a van and can't even park it by the river and I have no friends.	Earn more now Automate savings Actively manage my health, finances, work skills, and my connections so I find work more easily in the future	Get a new job or new side work Stay with friends Work somewhere that has room and board covered	If I don't take action around my fears, I will avoid risks that I should be taking or take lucrative but unfulfilling work that leads to regret, and diminished sense of self.

How Interesting

I recently began using "How Interesting".

When things don't go the way you planned, the way you want or expect, not on your schedule, etc. one chooses to react with "How Interesting". This reply leaves space for new interpretations. The thing or event may still not be what you wanted, but there might be a chance to be able to hold multiple beliefs at once about a topic. It reminds me of a Tony Robbins prompt to always ask what could be good about this awful thing? This phrase may give you the space to then use a cognitive reframe.

How Interesting

Cognitive Reframing

The next model I love is cognitive reframing. For me, this felt like magic the first time I tried it. Cognitive reframing allows you to transform a fear or a belief into a new, more empowering belief or truth. Mine are on my phone's wallpaper and the bathroom mirror. It almost feels like cheating when you do this! This book wouldn't be in your hands without cognitive reframing. It can be powerful to consider where you got each of these beliefs that may be limiting you, so you can further convince yourself that you can let go of it now if it doesn't serve you well.

My Fear or Belief	My New Belief/ What's the opposite of my fear or belief?	What are at least 3 things that prove the New Belief?
e.g. I won't finish this book	I will write and finish this book because it is so important to do	I have scheduled blocks of writing time on my calendar, so I work with fewer interruptions. I have set deadlines with others, so I'll scramble to finish, and give up perfectionism. I told many people this is coming and it's awkward to not deliver. I can swap writing for unessential TV. I am collaborating with friends who ask about progress I am getting help on the parts of the process that were less familiar and made me uncomfortable.

Getting Unstuck In Relationships

While all of the above help in relationships, here are a few more tools for getting unstuck in relationship issues specifically.

Drucker's Dependencies

> ## "Who do I depend on for what?
>
> ## Who depends on me for what?"
>
> -Peter Drucker

This quote from Peter Drucker, the inventor of management theory, is one of my favorites that almost always helps to reduce conflict. He recommends revisiting these questions for each person in your life each year, and anytime you experience a major change. This process of thinking about and describing dependencies to each other identifies mismatches in expectations that are better to catch early.

I have never worked anywhere where there was not a mismatch of expectations about responsibilities across departments and teams. Working overseas, I discovered that Americans understood an Operations Manager's role to be the unenviable job of making sure the technology infrastructure and processes are effective, efficient, scaling well and to be at work at 3 a.m. if there is an outage. For my Irish colleagues, an Operations Manager is a Senior Management role that would never be in the weeds of troubleshooting at 3am. All of us were a bit surprised by this discrepancy in understanding when I articulated it after using this tool.

At home, it uncovered a difference of expectations that I summarize as "I am not upset about the division of labor, I am upset by the lack of division of labor" and articulating it has helped make things less unbalanced.

Relationship and Family Systems Thinking experts have more good ideas I've been using.

Bowen Systems Thinking

Bowen Systems Theory describes the predictable patterns in families and groups and encourages taking responsibility for managing yourself, your life and your reactions to make your life better and improve the whole social system.

Therapist Glennon Gordon has a great summary on how to strengthen relationships

1. **Observe the whole system:** Become an expert in your own family. Notice what happens when your husband is speaking to your child. Observe what happens in the family when you're in a bad mood or in a good mood. What goes on inside of you when your partner is in a good or bad mood?
2. **Focus on your part:** Take accountability for how your functioning contributes to the process in the family. Spend a whole day only paying attention to your reactivity and how you may affect people around you. Experiment with doing something different and watch what happens.
3. **Know what the patterns are:** Conflict, distancing, over/under functioning, triangulating. Learn the dance. When she does this, I do that; when I do this, he reacts that way. By knowing the pattern, you have more choice in your part.
4. **Make focused choices to do things differently**: If you have observed that when she gets angry you distance, make a choice to stay in it. You are successfully making a focused choice to do it a little differently, it empowers you and shifts the reactivity pattern.
5. **Keep working on becoming more of a self:** Yes, you are part of a team, but a team is only as good as the sum of its parts. Always be working on the answer to what do I think, what do I believe, what is important to me?[7]

---

[7] https://www.instagram.com/p/B3U7AeZB4Py/

Observe the whole system, what patterns do you see?

Focus on your part: how do you react?

How can you change your responses to be more of a self, more independent?

Author Andrea Schara, in her book **Your Mindful Compass: Breakthrough Strategies for Navigating Life/Work Relationships in any Social Jungle** describes how Bowen Theory extends beyond the family and into society. "When anxiety goes up in society or in families there is a togetherness-oriented, other-focused, blaming behavior, which is precisely the opposite of the effort to figure out answers for oneself. More mature people say, "What can I change about me to deal with them or to deal with this situation?"[8]

---

[8] https://yourmindfulcompass.com/2011/05/12/be-a-self-or-be-swept-away-regula-tors-of-behavior-in-social-systems/

Divorce trends amplify the importance of healing relationships

It is important to note trends because divorce can be one of the largest risks to thriving.

Grey divorce, divorce by people who are 50 and older, has doubled since 1990 and tripled for people over 65.[9] Susan Brown and the National Center for Family & Marriage Research has shown the standard of living declines 45% for women who divorce after age fifty (twice the amount of earlier studies) and 21% for older men (versus negligible declines for younger men). Even hedge fund managers are off their game for up to two years after divorce.[10] Grey divorce can be awful emotionally for an entire family but also a huge financial risk for retirement and solvency later in life.

The best way to recover from grey divorce, is to find a new partner. Depression increases for about 4 years after a divorce versus 8 years after being widowed. "Remarrying or re-partnering will end depression almost immediately."[11]

Financially, over 50 and married, remarried, or cohabiting couples have poverty rates of 4% or less compared to divorcees over 50, with 11% of men and 27 % of women in poverty.[12]

For younger people the impact is even greater because the lifetime trajectory of savings is reduced. Motley Fool cites a **77% drop in wealth for all ages of divorcees, which varied little between genders**, due in part to division of assets and maintaining separate households.[13]

---

[9] https://www.kiplinger.com/article/retirement/t065-c032-s014-the-true-cost-of-gray-divorce.html
[10] https://www.latimes.com/business/story/2019-07-19/divorce-destroys-finances-of-americans-over-50
[11] https://www.latimes.com/business/story/2019-07-19/divorce-destroys-finances-of-americans-over-50
[12] https://www.survivedivorce.com/gray-divorce
[13] https://www.fool.com/the-ascent/research/average-cost-of-divorce/

3- What makes people happy in general?

Fantastic! Now that you've layered your why you want to change with new beliefs and fear setting and ways of being more of a self and better addressing relationship stuck-ness, we come to the happy data. This chapter has no tables to fill in, only a summary of lots of research so you can avoid other peoples' mistakes.

Here's what we cover in this section:

- ▶ What is happiness?
- ▶ Essentials to consider and how to decide among them
- ▶ How happiness varies across the US
- ▶ How costs vary across the US
- ▶ Working in retirement
- ▶ Timing - You may not need to wait to make a change.

What is Happiness?

Let's look a little more at what makes up happiness. I love the summary of happiness in this joke.

What did the Monk say to the hot dog vendor?

Make me one with everything.

That joke distills the essence of happiness and what people are looking for - it has both the immediate pleasure (of eating a snack) and the sense of larger purpose and meaning, life fulfilment, and connection.

How much of happiness is under your control?

"Happiness is not something that comes readymade. It comes from your own actions"

-Dalai Lama

In her book **The How of Happiness,** Sonja Lyubomirsky calls attention to the 40% slice of pie; "This much is in your power to change".

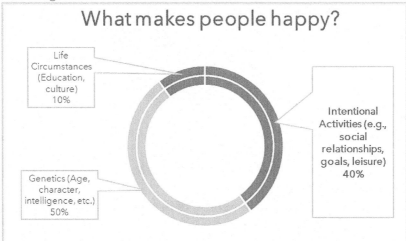

What makes people happy?

Life Circumstances (Education, culture) 10%

Intentional Activities (e.g., social relationships, goals, leisure) 40%

Genetics (Age, character, intelligence, etc.) 50%

The Essentials

The largest contributors to happiness are having basic needs met, social connection, and having a sense of purpose and meaning. These are the essential or critical elements.

Health, money, being in a place you love, many other things can all contribute to happiness, but are not prerequisites for happiness. Work and leisure can fulfill these happiness needs. Your priorities should include your own preferences that lead to your happiness and in the next chapter we'll cover how to uncover those. First, let's look at each of the contributors to happiness.

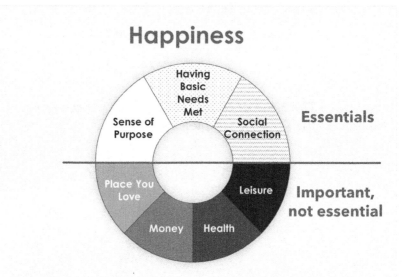

Having Basic Needs Met

Happiness expert and inventor of the field, Ed Diener says "Having your basic needs met is a pillar of well-being."[14]

[14] http://labs.psychology.illinois.edu/~ediener/discoveries.html

Happiness expert Sonja Lyubomirsky defines basic needs as food, shelter, and safety.[15]

Maslow's Hierarchy of Needs is another way to think about human needs, often depicted on a pyramid with basic needs such as food and water at the base, leading up safety, love, esteem, and self-fulfillment or actualization at the top. "According to Maslow, when a lower need is met, the next need on the hierarchy becomes our focus of attention."[16]

The recent book and YouTube videos by Helen Russell, author of **The Year of Living Danishly: Uncovering the Secrets of the World's Happiest Country**, observes that neither the US nor the UK provide security and stability in work or healthcare and only lead their citizens to the second tier on Maslow's hierarchy of needs. Denmark is the World's Happiest Country because it gets its citizens to the top of the hierarchy pyramid with surprising things like paid time off for education to change careers and providing education for free. Because their basic needs are taken care of, Denmark's citizens are happier.[17]

Social Connection
Social connections include all relationships & friends. Having close friends and a network of social support has a distinct positive effect on happiness, to such a degree that some scholars have suggested that this could be the single most important source of happiness. In a study of very happy people, every single one of them had excellent social relationships. Other studies document that those who enjoy close relationships are better at coping with major life stresses such as bereavement, rape, unemployment, and illness. Perceived loneliness is robustly linked to depression.[18] Stanford's

---

[15] https://www.bluezones.com/2012/07/work-hard-play-hard-9-questions-for-sonja-lyubomirsky/

[16] Hopper, Elizabeth. "Maslow's Hierarchy of Needs Explained." ThoughtCo, Aug. 18, 2021, https://thoughtco.com/maslows-hierarchy-of-needs-4582571 .

[17] https://www.youtube.com/watch?v=h1RXGltx4SI

[18] Diener, Ed and Kesebir, Pelin and Tov, William, Happiness (2009). Handbook of Individual Differences in Social Behavior, pp. 147-160, M. Leary & R. Hoyle, eds., Guilford Press, 2009 , Available at SSRN: https://ssrn.com/abstract=2143374

Longevity research indicates 97% of people cited social connectedness as the primary factor affecting quality of life[19]

- Friends matter most if you're single or if unhappily married (partnered)
- Happy marriage and partners are key
- Family relationships help but not nearly as much as partners and friends
- Having kids has no bearing on happiness later in life, on average

How important is social connection? In a book by Marta Zaraska, Growing Young: How Friendship, Optimism, and Kindness Can Help You Live to 100. The quote that caught my eye: "Studies show that building a **strong support network of family and friends lowers mortality risk by about 45%**. Exercise, on the other hand, can lower that risk by 23 to 33%."[20]

Marta Zaraska also emphasizes this is that this is scientifically proven.

> "Another thing I haven't realized before is how directly our social lives and our mental habits affect our physiology. Sometimes people ask me if it isn't some kind of new-agey stuff. It definitely isn't. There are so many various research studies showing effects of these "soft drivers" on health: epidemiological studies, randomized experiments, studies on animals, on cell cultures, and so on, showing effects on gene expression, on the levels of immune proteins in the blood, on our hormones, brain activation patterns, etc. We are talking about strictly biological effects here."[21]

My vote is to combine exercise with a friend in the name of longevity.

[19] https://longevity.stanford.edu/sightlines-project-social-engagement-special-report/
[20] https://www.bluezones.com/2020/10/this-may-be-the-untold-secret-to-longevity-hint-its-not-only-what-you-eat
[21] https://www.bluezones.com/2020/10/this-may-be-the-untold-secret-to-longevity-hint-its-not-only-what-you-eat

Additional attributes of social connection to consider:

Marriage

Married people tend to be happier, but if you are not happily married it is worse than being single, despite the possibility of higher income. [22]

Children & Family

Research from Ed Diener et al shows that first born children increase their parents' happiness; additional children reduce their mothers' happiness; leaving fathers' happiness unchanged in the US. "Another remarkable finding from their study was that having had children at one point in their lives did not have any effect on the happiness level of men and women at ages 50-70.[23]

" The number of other family does not seem to matter, but there is evidence to suggest a positive relation between the degree of contact with other family members and life satisfaction. [24]

Caregiving

While family may be dear to you, caregiving can be a substantial cost and impact to your career, health, and happiness especially if you yourself have health challenges or are caring for someone with dementia. "Retirees who provide family care but are not engaged in other volunteer or work

[22] Finke, Michael S. and Ho, Nhat and Huston, Sandra J., Spending, Relationship Quality, and Life Satisfaction in Retirement (September 23, 2017). 2018 Academic Research Colloquium for Financial Planning and Related Disciplines, Available at SSRN: https://ssrn.com/abstract=3041761 or http://dx.doi.org/10.2139/ssrn.3041761
[23] Diener, Ed and Kesebir, Pelin and Tov, William, Happiness (2009). Handbook of Individual Differences in Social Behavior, pp. 147-160, M. Leary & R. Hoyle, eds., Guilford Press, 2009, Available at SSRN: https://ssrn.com/abstract=2143374
[24] Finke, Michael S. and Ho, Nhat and Huston, Sandra J., Spending, Relationship Quality, and Life Satisfaction in Retirement (September 23, 2017). 2018 Academic Research Colloquium for Financial Planning and Related Disciplines, Available at SSRN: https://ssrn.com/abstract=3041761 or http://dx.doi.org/10.2139/ssrn.3041761

activities are much less likely than other older adults to be satisfied with their retirement.[25]

Sex

Per a 2004 paper, sex does make people happier. A typical American has sex 2-3x/month but 1/3 of Americans over 40 say they are celibate. Married people have more sex. The happiness-maximizing number of sexual partners in the previous year is 1. Homosexuality has no statistically significant effect on happiness.[26]

Religion

Pew Research found religious people are 10% more likely to describe themselves as very happy compared to unreligious people.[27]

Purpose

Transamerica Center for Retirement Studies found that 97% of retirees are happier because they have a strong sense of purpose.[28] People with a sense of purpose live an average of 7.5 years longer.[29] "People do many things because they are deemed purposeful or worthwhile, even if they are not especially pleasurable (e.g., reading the same story over and over again to a child, visiting a sick friend, or volunteering); they also do many things that are pleasant even if they are not viewed as having much long-term meaning in the imagined

---

[25] Johnson, Richard Warren and Lo Sasso, Anthony T., Parental Care at Midlife: Balancing Work and Family Responsibilities Near Retirement (March 2000). Available at SSRN: https://ssrn.com/abstract=260259 or http://dx.doi.org/10.2139/ssrn.260259
[26] Blanchflower, David G. and Oswald, Andrew J., Money, Sex, and Happiness: An Empirical Study (May 2004). NBER Working Paper No. w10499, Available at SSRN: https://ssrn.com/abstract=552104
[27] https://www.pewresearch.org/fact-tank/2019/01/31/are-religious-people-happier-healthier-our-new-global-study-explores-this-question/
[28] https://medium.com/authority-magazine/5-things-retirees-say-they-wish-they-were-told-before-they-began-retirement-with-patti-black-c725eed41319
[29] https://www.nextavenue.org/insights-on-ageism/

future."[30] Research shows unambiguously that making progress toward meaningful goals is important to thrive.[31]

Why continuing to work past retirement age might be a good idea for your happiness

Research from Merrill Lynch & Age Wave shows the retirement model is changing - we keep working; we have multiple stages of retirement and work, and we aren't doing it just for the money. This has been driven by economic uncertainty, fewer pensions, increasing life expectancy and a revisioning of what later life should look like.

If social connection, sense of purpose, health and wealth are all improved by working at something you enjoy, you can see why 72% of those over age 50 want to continue to work. Nearly three out of five retirees launch into a new line of work, and working retirees are three times more likely than pre-retirees to be entrepreneurs.[32]

Retirees are increasingly likely to start their own businesses, "26% of retirees became entrepreneurs in 2017 vs 15% 20 years earlier."[33] The availability of Medicare later in life removes the challenge and expense of healthcare.

---

[30] National Research Council 2013. Subjective Well-Being: Measuring Happiness, Suffering, and Other Dimensions of Experience. Washington, DC: The National Academies Press. https://doi.org/10.17226/18548.

[31] Diener, Ed and Kesebir, Pelin and Tov, William, Happiness (2009). Handbook of Individual Differences in Social Behavior, pp. 147-160, M. Leary & R. Hoyle, eds., Guilford Press, 2009, Available at SSRN: https://ssrn.com/abstract=2143374

[32] Per the Merrill Lynch and Age Wave national study, *Work in Retirement: Myths and Motivations.* https://agewave.com/what-we-do/landmark-research-and-consulting/research-studies/work-and-retirement-myths-and-motivations/

[33] https://www.bloomberg.com/news/articles/2019-09-20/retirees-are-becoming-new-entrepreneurs

WORKING RETIREES

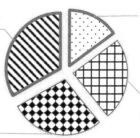

Caring Contributors (33%)
seek to give back to their communities or worthwhile causes. Four out of ten work for a nonprofit, and more than a quarter are unpaid volunteers.

Earnest Earners (28%)
need the income from working in retirement to pay the bills. Fewer are satisfied or motivated at work.

Driven Achievers (15%)
four out of five (79%) feel at the top of their game, 39% own a business or are self-employed. They are the most satisfied with work, and they tend to be workaholics, even in retirement.

Life Balancers (24%)
primarily want to keep working for the workplace friendships and social connections—and for the extra money. They seek work that is fun and not stressful, and often work part-time.

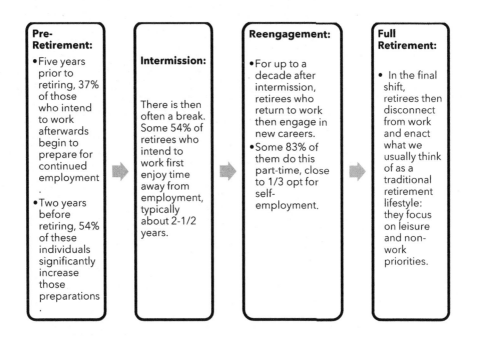

Pre-Retirement:
- Five years prior to retiring, 37% of those who intend to work afterwards begin to prepare for continued employment.
- Two years before retiring, 54% of these individuals significantly increase those preparations.

Intermission:

There is then often a break. Some 54% of retirees who intend to work first enjoy time away from employment, typically about 2-1/2 years.

Reengagement:
- For up to a decade after intermission, retirees who return to work then engage in new careers.
- Some 83% of them do this part-time, close to 1/3 opt for self-employment.

Full Retirement:
- In the final shift, retirees then disconnect from work and enact what we usually think of as a traditional retirement lifestyle: they focus on leisure and non-work priorities.

Anthropologist Mary Catherine Bateson describes life and aging as an improvisation akin to creating a quilt from disparate pieces. In ***Composing A Further Life: The Age of Active Wisdom*** she describes people entering a second adulthood and finding "new meaning and ways to contribute, composing their lives in new patterns."[34]

Important but not prerequisite

Money
Once basic needs are met, money is no longer a prerequisite for happiness.

Happiness is feeling at a point in time, life satisfaction is a sense one gets reflecting over a lifetime. Daniel Kahneman and Angus Deaton are known for their work showing wealth

---

[34] Bateson, Mary Catherine ***Composing A Life: Life As A Work In Progress -The Improvisations of Five Extraordinary Women.*** New York, Plume, 1989

contributes to happiness only up to a point and that it impacts life satisfaction more. "Income and education are more closely related to life evaluation, but health, care giving, loneliness, and smoking are relatively stronger predictors of daily emotions. Emotional well-being also rises with log income, but there is no further progress beyond an annual income of ~$75,000. Low income exacerbates the emotional pain associated with such misfortunes as divorce, ill health, and being alone. High income buys life satisfaction but not happiness, and that low income is associated both with low life evaluation and low emotional well-being."[35]

In 2021, the Washington Post reported that this long held maxim that money doesn't buy happiness is no longer true. "The link [between income and happiness] is stronger now than in previous decades, the decrease in happiness among lower-income people may be a result of rising inequality, increasing real estate values and decreased ability to pay for education."[36]

Having money increases the likelihood of happiness but it is neither a guarantee nor a prerequisite for happiness.

Poverty

Poverty[37] has been shown to reduce happiness and poverty rates vary widely across the US, per US Census data.[38]. In retirement age: Blacks, Hispanics, and single women face a higher poverty rate than other seniors. Poverty rates for

[35] High income improves evaluation of life but not emotional well-being Daniel Kahneman, Angus Deaton Proceedings of the National Academy of Sciences Sep 2010, 107 (38) 16489-16493; DOI: 10.1073/pnas.1011492107 Available at https://www.pnas.org/content/107/38/16489

[36] https://www.washingtonpost.com/local/social-issues/money-can-buy-happiness/2020/07/01/3c2fc554-bb5a-11ea-8cf5-9c1b8d7f84c6_story.html

[37] Blanchflower, David G. and Oswald, Andrew J., Unhappiness and Pain in Modern America: A Review Essay, and Further Evidence, on Carol Graham's Happiness for All?. IZA Discussion Paper No. 11184, Available at SSRN: https://ssrn.com/abstract=3081418

[38] https://factfinder.census.gov/faces/nav/jsf/pages/download_center.xhtml#none - Selected 2017 ACS 5-year data for All Metropolitan Statistical Areas US and PR

women are nearly double that of men for almost all Census survey years.[39]

Leisure

Leisure activities such as music, exercise, and reading significantly contribute to happiness. People who work fewer hours have been demonstrated to have higher life satisfaction.[40]

Spending time in nature is good for you. We know that walking on quiet, tree-lined paths can result in meaningful improvements to mental health, and even physical changes to the brain. Natural light exposure – by spending time outside or living in a space with natural light – is good for your mood.[41]

Health

Like money, health is a basic need and pillar of well-being, and like money it helps but is not necessary as a prerequisite to happiness. Being healthy contributes to wealth, relationships and happiness and vice versa.

"People who suffer life-threatening illnesses, which interfere with their daily life and cause pain, are known to be less happy. However, researchers find weak and sometimes nonexistent correlations between happiness and objective health as assessed by medical personnel. The associations between happiness and subjective health—as it is reported by the individual—are consistently strong. It is not clear if objective health measures are sometimes not as objective as one would hope or if subjective reports of health reflect emotional adjustments on the part of the person."[42] **Research also**

[39] Banerjee, Sudipto, Time Trends in Poverty for Older Americans between 2001-2009 (April 1, 2012). EBRI Notes, Vol. 33, No. 4, April 2012, Available at SSRN: https://ssrn.com/abstract=2046720
[40] Diener, Ed and Kesebir, Pelin and Tov, William, Happiness (2009). Handbook of Individual Differences in Social Behavior, pp. 147-160, M. Leary & R. Hoyle, eds., Guilford Press, 2009, Available at SSRN: https://ssrn.com/abstract=2143374
[41] Parker-Pope, Tara How to Be Happy - Well Guides - The New York Times https://www.nytimes.com/guides/well/how-to-be-happy
[42] Diener, Ed and Kesebir, Pelin and Tov, William, Happiness (2009). Handbook of Individual Differences in Social Behavior, pp. 147-160, M. Leary & R. Hoyle, eds., Guilford Press, 2009, Available at SSRN: https://ssrn.com/abstract=2143374

consistently shows terminally ill people are more positive than those not facing death.

Mental Health & Well-being improves health

Reporting being happier is associated with being healthier, living longer, having better relationships and even increased productivity. Daily stress increases illness and reduced well-being is a likely causal factor for some health outcomes."[43] Mental Health impacts overall life satisfaction as well as short term happiness.

"Mental health is the biggest single predictor of life-satisfaction. It explains more of the variance of life-satisfaction in the population of a country than physical health does, and much more than unemployment and income do. Income explains 1% of the variance of life-satisfaction or less. The most common forms of mental illness are depression and anxiety disorders. Rigorously defined, these affect about 10% of all the world's population – and prevalence is similar in rich and poor countries. Depression and anxiety are more common during working age than in later life. "[44]

The pandemic has doubled those rates in the US as of June 2020[45] Those rates seem to have leveled off in more recent months per The USC Center for Economic and Social Research's Understanding Coronavirus in America.[46]

Wealth lead to health but health leads to wealth

Health leads to wealth in later years because it impacts productivity and wages over one's lifetime. Early childhood poor living conditions are predictors of disease later in life. Mental health can have immediate causal effect on wealth,

---

[43] National Research Council 2013. Subjective Well-Being: Measuring Happiness, Suffering, and Other Dimensions of Experience. Washington, DC: The National Academies Press. https://doi.org/10.17226/18548.

[44] https://www.iza.org/publications/dp/7620/mental-illness-and-unhappiness

[45] https://worldhappiness.report/ed/2021/mental-health-and-the-covid-19-pandemic/

[46] https://covid19pulse.usc.edu/

physical health's causal effects on wealth are visible a few years later. Increased wealth leads to an increase in quality of healthcare. "The evidence indicates good health improves wealth but there is little evidence to show wealth leads to better health."[47]

Poverty & Health

Poverty[48] has been shown to reduce happiness and varies widely across the US per Census data.[49]. The chance of suffering a health condition (acute or otherwise) rose 45-55 percent for those below the poverty line.[50]

Retirement impacts health and happiness

Research data shows health issues increase in retirement including a 5-16% increase in difficulties with mobility, 5-6% increase in illness and 6-9% decline in mental health per six-year period after retirement. Decreases in physical activity and social interaction are correlated with this decrease in health. Being married, having social support, physical activity and continuing to work part-time in retirement mitigates these adverse health effects.[51]

The research of Laura Carstensen, a psychology professor and director of Stanford University's Center on Longevity finds that positive emotions increase and negative emotions decrease over time among those in or near retirement.

---

[47] Michaud, Pierre-Carl and van Soest, Arthur H. O., Health and Wealth of Elderly Couples: Causality Tests Using Dynamic Panel Data Models (September 2004). IZA Discussion Paper No. 1312; CentER Discussion Paper No. 2004-81, Available at SSRN: https://ssrn.com/abstract=594846

[48] Blanchflower, David G. and Oswald, Andrew J., Unhappiness and Pain in Modern America: A Review Essay, and Further Evidence, on Carol Graham's Happiness for All?. IZA Discussion Paper No. 11184, Available at SSRN: https://ssrn.com/abstract=3081418

[49] https://factfinder.census.gov/faces/nav/jsf/pages/download_center.xhtml#none - Selected 2017 ACS 5-year data for All Metropolitan Statistical Areas US and PR

[50] Banerjee, Sudipto, Time Trends in Poverty for Older Americans between 2001-2009 (April 1, 2012). EBRI Notes, Vol. 33, No. 4, April 2012, Available at SSRN: https://ssrn.com/abstract=2046720

[51] Dave, Dhaval and Kelly, Inas and Spasojevic, Jasmina, The Effects of Retirement on Physical and Mental Health Outcomes (October 2007). Andrew Young School of Policy Studies Research Paper Series No. 07-35, Available at SSRN: https://ssrn.com/abstract=1024475 or http://dx.doi.org/10.2139/ssrn.1024475

- 72% of retirees say they are "extremely or quite happy," versus 61% of pre-retirees.
- ~70% of retiree's report being "extremely or quite relaxed," versus 34% of pre-retirees.
- Pre-retirement worries fade with 44 % of pre-retirees worried about financial uncertainty versus 31% of retirees who say that has been an issue.
- 14% of retirees worry about how to fill their time versus 31% of those still working
- As retirement progresses, satisfaction rises. Among those who retired less than five years ago, 56% report being satisfied versus 63% who retired more than five years ago."[52]

Where you live
A place you love is helpful: moving might be a good idea per Dan Buettner, National Geographic Journalist, author of The Blue Zones of Happiness.

"If you're unhappy, you don't just need a new attitude. You need a moving van."[53]

-Dan Buettner

Happiness varies more than you'd expect across the US

The WalletHub map of the Happiest States in the U.S. below shows happiness varies widely. "In order to determine the happiest states in America, WalletHub compared the 50 states across three key dimensions: 1) Emotional & Physical Well-

---

[52] https://www.nextavenue.org/retirement-just-might-pay-you-happiness-bonus/
[53] https://www.inc.com/jessica-stillman/he-studied-worlds-happiest-places-for-15-years-this-is-no-1-thing-he-learned.html

Being, 2) Work Environment and 3) Community & Environment. We evaluated those dimensions using 32 relevant metrics."[54]

Main Findings

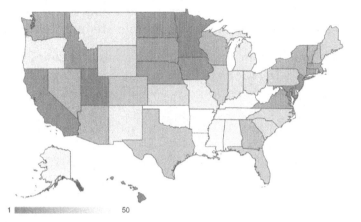

The average score was 52, and the range was from 33 in WV to the happiest, 68, in HI. (Darker colors are happier) Across some of the metrics, depression differences between most and least depressed states varied 2X. Most and least safe states varied 50X.

Clearly, one can be happy anywhere, but the research of happiness distills lessons learned from the happiest cities and places in America (and around the world):

- **Openness**: People are happy when they live in a community that is welcoming to all.[51]
- **Beauty**: Living in a scenic, community, with lots of trees and green space, makes people happier.[51]
- **Social opportunities**: When a community is designed to foster social connections – restaurants, community spaces, sidewalks, trails for walking and biking, parks and other public spaces – people are happier.[55],[52]

[54] https://wallethub.com/edu/best-and-worst-cities-for-an-active-lifestyle/8817/
[55] Parker-Pope, Tara How to Be Happy - Well Guides - The New York Times https://www.nytimes.com/guides/well/how-to-be-happy

- **Improving Access to Good Food** Reducing fast food and junk food consumption and making fruits and vegetables cheaper and more accessible makes for happier, healthier residents. [52]
- **Taking care of needy people:** When communities have good health care, good education, and quality social services for everyone, people are happier.[56]

A recent article from TrendWatching about the year 2021[57] describes 15-MINUTE CITIES as an innovative way of creating happier cities.

"US startup Reef is on a mission to build 15-minute cities' where everything people need can be found within a short walk or bicycle ride. To this end, Reef is transforming its real estate network of more than 4,500 parking lots and garages into neighborhood hubs. It's partnering with other players for micro-fulfillment, e-bikes, pop-up clinics and urban farming. We're steadily moving towards people-first, car-free urban environments that prioritize wellbeing."

[56& 17] https://www.bluezones.com/2017/10/happiness-lessons-from-happiest-countries-and-cities-in-the-world/
[57] http://info.trendwatching.com/21-trends-for-2021

Costs vary less than you'd expect across the US

US Wide Summary

	Household Income before taxes	Average Annual Expenditure	Average Annual Expenditures as % of Pre-Tax Income	Food	Food % of Pre-Tax Income	Housing	Housing % of Pre-Tax Income
US Min	$61,380	$50,622	73%	$6,807	9.3%	$14,656	23.9%
US Max	$88,222	$69,981	91%	$9,166	11.9%	$24,582	27.9%
US Avg	$74,729	$59,989	81%	$7,752	10.4%	$19,536	26.1%
	Transportation	Transportation % of Pre-Tax Income	Health Care	Health % of Pre-Tax Income	Personal Taxes (Federal, State, Local & Other Taxes)	Personal Tax % of Income (Not including Property or other taxes)	
US Min	$9,046	10.3%	$4,600	5.2%	$7,261	11.2%	
US Max	$11,125	15.8%	$5,477	7.6%	$14,283	16.3%	
US Avg	$9,715	13.1%	$4,926	6.7%	$10,282	13.6%	

Source: Consumer Expenditure Survey, U.S. Bureau of Labor Statistics. September. 2019

Costs across the US vary less than you'd expect, per recent Bureau of Labor statistics.

Author and founder of BlueZones.com, Dan Buettner, succinctly describes the reality of money and happiness. "When you evaluate your life overall, money is important. Millionaires are generally happier than people who make $30,000 a year. But $75,000 is about the cap. If you make more than that, then your day-to-day experience doesn't get any better – you just have more stuff. This 75k marker is an average and is also on a sliding scale based on where you live (75k in NYC doesn't mean the same things that it means in a rural community)."[58]

Other criteria

Physical surroundings and the criteria which may matter to you are worth thinking about including population; rural, urban or suburban; college town, topography and landscape, presence of airports, local parks and other amenities.

Weather is known to impact your mood. Summer & winter length and temperatures are important, both long term and recent temperature trends. Having four seasons, or not, is often a strong preference. Precipitation, drought risk (Palmer Z), and the NOAA National Centers for Environmental information US Climate Extremes Index (CEI) may also be worth considering with climate change. Snowfall, sunshine, humidity, and heat are all noted to influence well-being.

If you have asthma, or other concerns about climate or climate change locally, then please download the **Free Climate Report** on my website to see local levels of air, water and land pollution, climate extremes index, asthma and cancer rates, pollution, topography, Climate Extremes index, temperatures, drought and wild fire risks and public health data.

Social Capital: Happiness researcher Stephan Goetz reports higher levels of happiness when people were subject to shorter commutes, moved homes less and lived in place with higher social capital (close-knit communities)."[59]

Housing: Maxwell Ryan's, founder of Apartment Therapy, observed while working as a teacher and doing home visits "children who came from well-designed, organized and healthy homes were the happiest, most productive and performed best in school. It had nothing to do with the size of the apartment or the finances of its owners." [60]

Architecture: In Alain de Botton's Architecture of Happiness videos and the book, he asks people to consider how they live,

---

[59] https://economicdevelopment.org/2014/12/the-geography-of-happiness-where-americans-are-happiest-and-why/

[60] https://businessofhome.com/articles/putting-the-therapy-in-apartment-therapy-with-maxwell-ryan

what is important to them, and designing housing that meets those needs rather than always defaulting to designs hundreds of years old. "Our lives are different than they were then and our interiors should be too."[61] He advocates for more light, more beauty, and neighborhood layouts that promote interaction. He describes how where you live influences who you are; in so many small and large profound ways.

"What we search for in a work of architecture is not in the end so far from what we search for in a friend."

-Alain de Botton

"At the AgingWell Hub's Spoken Hub discussion, Whitney Austin Gray, PhD, LEED AP examines how best to create environments where healthy aging in place is possible through innovative uses of architecture, design and technology. Dr. Gray provides an overview of the WELL Building standard and how it can be applied to ensure that the built environment promotes and supports efforts to live healthy lives."[62]

A few more notes about where you live

"Simplicity is an acquired taste. Mankind, left free, instinctively complicates life"

-Katharine Elizabeth Fullerton Gerould

After this quote about complicating life, I will smile and try to keep this book simpler. I offer a Selection Tool with 700+ attributes across 382 US places that is a dream for people who want lots of details, and saves research time, but may not simplify the process. I will add just a few points:

Unknowns You Might Be Missing Out On
There will likely be items you hadn't considered. There are surprises - like the number of independent and public radio

---

[61] https://www.alaindebotton.com/architecture/watch/
[62] Dr. Whitney Gray - Creating Environments to Enable Healthy Aging
https://vimeo.com/184006936

stations, that are not just for pleasure, but a critical public health issue. The New York times reported on a story of how commercial radio stations, across multiple states, failed to do emergency alerts during a toxic train derailment. The radio stations had been centralized and now one could be reached for several days to do the announcements. The result was hundreds injured and one person dead.[63]

Independent and public radio is often more prevalent where there is a vibrant live music scene and maybe another reason to consider this as you choose where to move.

Combinations & Interpretations of Criteria

In addition to missing unknowns, the combinations of criteria are also important to review.

For example, if considering moving and you're comparing Albuquerque and Asheville, NC - Albuquerque has low taxes, but Asheville has a lower overall cost of living in both absolute dollars and as a percentage of income. However, the number of doctors available per 100k of population is below the US average in Asheville; which might be important to you as you age. If you are look more, you'd see Baltimore has a below average cost of living, a high number of doctors, and a higher than US average life expectancy- and may well score higher than Albuquerque or Asheville, NC on your comparison. The data will surprise you, so don't let taxes or cost be the sole criteria to consider.

You'll also sometimes have to look at a wider set of criteria to make sense of data points. For instance, the number of people working after age 70 in the DC metro area is higher than the US average. However, the average income and percent unemployment are far lower than average. People may not be working late in life out of necessity but because there is opportunity and the difference between necessity and desire is huge.

---

[63] https://www.nytimes.com/2007/01/28/magazine/28WWLN_IdeaLab.t.html

You can become much more likely to move just by....
Planning to move!

Per the American Housing Survey 2019 by the U.S. Census Bureau:

- 27.7% of US households moved in the past 2 years
- 69% of those moving moved less than 50 miles
- 44% of movers reported increased housing costs, 23% decreased, 20% about the same

The long-term trends are:

- Wanting to move and expecting to move are separate things. Most people who say they would like to move do not. Most people who expect to move actually do move, whether they want to or not. **Expecting to move made people 8X more likely to actually move.**
- Experiencing any housing problems (such as noise, damp or a lack of space) increases desire to move. Having excess space in your house makes you less likely to desire a move.
- On average, a move is preceded by a significant decline in happiness. The boost from moving appears to bring people back to their long-term happiness level; moving is one of several means to regain a stable sense of well-being.
- People who move a long-distance are at least as happy as people who move only a short-distance, despite the higher social costs that are involved. [64]

[64] Coulter, Rory and van Ham, Maarten and Feijten, Peteke, A Longitudinal Analysis of Moving Desires, Expectations and Actual Moving Behavior. IZA Discussion Paper No. 5277, Available at SSRN: https://ssrn.com/abstract=1700446

You're

8X

more likely to
move if you are
planning rather
than just wanting
to move, so let's
get planning!

A recent Atlantic article quotes the author Melody Warnick's book **This Is Where You Belong.** She presents the evidence on moving and happiness and argues that a large part of the unhappiness people suffer at the outset of arriving in a new place can be mitigated or avoided with things like "actively exploring your new neighborhood, doing the things that made you happy in your old home, and socializing with new people."[65]

Additional data on happiness

Can you buy happiness?
Yes, partially. The three main ways per research:

1. **Investing in others can make one feel healthier and wealthier.** "Research demonstrating that people derive more satisfaction spending money on others than they do spending it on themselves spans poor and rich countries alike, as well as income levels. The authors show how this phenomenon extends over an extraordinary range of circumstances, from a Canadian college student purchasing a scarf for her mother to a Ugandan woman buying lifesaving malaria medication for a friend. Indeed, the benefits of giving emerge among children before the age of two. Investing in others can make individuals feel healthier and

---

[65] https://www.theatlantic.com/family/archive/2021/01/what-moving-house-can-do-your-happiness/617667/

wealthier, even if it means making yourself a little poorer to reap these benefits. One study shows that giving as little as $1 away can cause you to feel more flush." [66]

2. **Spending to save time**
3. **Spending for experiences** "[67]
4. I'll add a fourth one for autonomy that I've relied on, summarized by Rolf Dobelli "Fuck-you money refers to the savings that would allow you to quit your job at a moment's notice without ending up in dire financial straits. One year's salary, say. Fuck-you money is freedom. More important even than material independence is that fuck-you money allows you to see and think objectively."[68]

Race and happiness

Social scientist Carol Graham's book "**Happiness for All**?" analyzes Gallup data trends and finds that the happiness of White Americans has been decreasing for decades but Black Americans have been becoming happier over time and are now as happy as Whites. This change in happiness happened although income gaps persisted.[69]

Living in an area of high rates of income inequality reduces happiness[70] Trends in income inequality and race:

- Asians Americans have displaced Blacks Americans as the most economically divided (high income inequality) group in the U.S. with the top 10% of Asian Americans earnings 10.7 times higher than the bottom 10%

---

[66] https://www.gsb.stanford.edu/insights/research-can-money-buy-happiness
[67] https://www.gsb.stanford.edu/insights/research-can-money-buy-happiness
[68] Dobelli, Rolf, The Art of the Good Life: Clear Thinking for Business and a Better Life 2017, Pages 52-53
[69] Blanchflower, David G. and Oswald, Andrew J., Unhappiness and Pain in Modern America: A Review Essay, and Further Evidence, on Carol Graham's Happiness for All? IZA Discussion Paper No. 11184, Available at SSRN: https://ssrn.com/abstract=3081418
[70] Blanchflower, David G. and Oswald, Andrew J., Unhappiness and Pain in Modern America: A Review Essay, and Further Evidence, on Carol Graham's Happiness for All?. IZA Discussion Paper No. 11184, Available at SSRN: https://ssrn.com/abstract=3081418

compared to a ratio of 9.8 times for Black Americans, 7.8 times for White and Hispanic Americans
- The income gap between Americans at the top and the bottom of the income distribution widened 27% from 1970 to 2016. In 1970, Americans near the top had 6.9 times as much income as those near the bottom; in 2016 that rate was 8.7X[71]

Gender and happiness

The data varies on whether women have more happiness life satisfaction but it agrees that they do have higher levels of daily stress. Increasing wealth, education and age as well as living in urban areas increases the difference in happiness between men and women. Where women's rights are compromised, life satisfaction of women decreases.[72]

For men, work is a linchpin. "Men who have high job satisfaction are more likely to feel optimistic, happy, motivated, emotionally stable, in control, and confident. Job satisfaction is by far the strongest predictor of positivity, being around three times higher than the next strongest predictor in every region and across the U.S. overall."[73]

There are few transgender happiness studies, but Sven Mueller is cited by the journal Nature for his work looking for hormonal and neurological links to mental health and gender identity.

"Depression rates are exceedingly high in people who do not identify with the gender they were assigned at birth, and as many as 30% of transgender teenagers attempt suicide. Societal acceptance and support can improve mental health, and although depression rates drop after treatment, the levels of depression and suicide are still above normal. "[74]

[71] https://www.pewresearch.org/social-trends/2018/07/12/income-inequality-in-the-u-s-is-rising-most-rapidly-among-asians/
[72] https://www.brookings.edu/essay/are-women-happier-than-men-do-gender-rights-make-a-difference/
[73] https://www.inc.com/bill-murphy-jr/a-massive-new-study-of-5000-men-says-this-1-very-surprising-thing-predicts-happiness.html from https://malepsychology.org.uk/research-library/
[74] https://www.nature.com/articles/d41586-019-01237-z

Impacts of the COVID Pandemic
Thriving in the Pandemic

Mental health is a bigger predictor of life satisfaction than physical health, unemployment, or income.[75] Mental health depressive symptoms increased from 9.7% of American adults from July 2019-Mar 2020 to 19.2% in June 2020.[76] Depression rates seem to have leveled off in more recent months per **The USC Center for Economic and Social Research's Understanding Coronavirus in America** report.[77]

A recent Life Evaluation Index published by Gallup Organization shows that while life satisfaction declined 10% in April 2020 to 46.4%, it has surged since. As of June 2021, American life satisfaction reached 59.2%, the highest in over 13 years.[78] Commuting tends to make people less happy. Stimulus checks made meeting basic needs easier for some. The impact on working parents was profound and often challenging also. The question for the future is how will happiness change again as people have more social contact, unemployment benefits end and more people return to their work places.

Health and access to health care discrepancies are apparent

Per the Centers for Disease Control,

"Health equity is when all members of society enjoy a fair and just opportunity to be as healthy as possible. Public health policies and programs centered around the specific needs of communities can promote health equity.

The COVID-19 pandemic has brought social and racial injustice and inequity to the forefront of public health. It has highlighted that health equity is still not a reality as COVID-19 has unequally affected many racial and ethnic minority groups, putting them more at risk of getting sick and dying from COVID-19. The term

---

[75] https://www.iza.org/publications/dp/7620/mental-illness-and-unhappiness
[76] https://worldhappiness.report/ed/2021/mental-health-and-the-covid-19-pandemic/
[77] https://covid19pulse.usc.edu/
[78] https://news.gallup.com/poll/351932/americans-life-ratings-reach-record-high.aspx

47

"racial and ethnic minority groups" includes people of color with a wide variety of backgrounds and experiences. Negative experiences are common to many people within these groups, and some social determinants of health have historically prevented them from having fair opportunities for economic, physical, and emotional health. Social determinants of health are the conditions in the places where people live, learn, work, play, and worship that affect a wide range of health risks and outcomes."[79]

Social Capital and the spread of COVID

There is a new Social Capital Index that is valuable to measure how tight knit a community is. The US Senate publishes the Social Capital Index data by State and County levels which you can download for free. It is worth reviewing as you decide where to move.[80]

The metrics on social capital's impact on COVID indicate the median US county has roughly 565 infections per 100,000 people, while counties in the 90th percentile have nearly five-times as many infections, even including controls for demographic characteristics.[81]

Moving rates

Has COVID made you more likely to move? The COVID Pandemic does mean remote work options are more plentiful than ever and more people are moving; mostly it is young people moving back home with family.[82] 44% of people are dissatisfied with their home since the pandemic[83]- so the moving trend is likely to continue.

Your likelihood of moving depends on your age. Prior to COVID, roughly 9% of Americans migrated every year, per

---

[79] https://www.cdc.gov/coronavirus/2019-ncov/community/health-equity/race-ethnicity.html
[80] https://www.lee.senate.gov/public/index.cfm/scp-index#:
[81] http://dx.doi.org/10.2139/ssrn.3592180
[82] https://www.cbsnews.com/news/coronavirus-moving-young-people-parents-relocation/
[83] https://magazine.realtor/daily-news/2020/10/01/44-of-owners-dissatisfied-with-home-since-pandemic

Census metrics, the lowest since data collection began 73 years ago.[84] We don't have 2020-2021 Census metrics yet, but a recent Move.org article based on a survey by Pollfish indicates the rates may be as high as 20% during 2020 (45% of those due to COVID and 33% not planned for the year) and are likely to increase another 20% in 2021. [85]

So, yes Americans overall are more likely to move since the pandemic began, but it is surprising to note how the rates vary by age category.

Percentage of people who moved this year (As a % of Total US Population)

Age Group	Census Data Pre COVID 2019-2020	Move.org Data During COVID in 2020	Estimated Increase in People who've moved this year with COVID (% of Total US Population)
<18 years old	2%	Not reported	N/A
18-24	2%	3%	1%
25-34	2%	7%	5%
35-44	1%	6%	5%
45-54	1%	2%	1%
54+	1%	1%	0%
Total All Ages	9%	20%	

If you use Move.org's percentages of movers per age group and the US 2020 population per the Census Bureau of 321,620,000 citizens to extrapolate % of total US population moving per age group this year we see very different trends by age. *If you're over the age of 54 you are not more likely to move. Younger people are more likely to move.* Of course, your own personal motivations and life events will influence your likelihood of moving.

---

[84] https://www.census.gov/topics/population/migration/data/tables.html
[85] https://www.move.org/2020-moving-stats-and-trends/

COVID And Work

The notable changes were

- Global GDP is estimated to have decreased by ~5% in 2020.[86]
- Nearly half of retirees left the workforce before their target retirement age and COVID-19 has accelerated this trend.[87]
- 62% of workers with at least a bachelor's degree can telework versus 23% with less education.[88]
- About 80% of those not teleworking report at least some in person interaction and 52% saying a lot of interaction. 50% are concerned about this potential exposure to COVID-19 but largely satisfied with the steps taken by employers to protect them.
- 70% of people work from home at least part of the time compared to 20% pre pandemic. 54% want to keep working from home after the pandemic.[89]
- For those fortunate to be able to do remote work, 451 Research reports 80% of organizations had expanded work from home policies by June 2020 and 67% expect them to remain long term or indefinitely.[90]

Consumer Price Index and Inflation during the pandemic to date

People often speak of inflation as if it were a single variable, as if 5% inflation applied to all things across all of the US. That isn't really true. You may have noticed this. The pandemic has exaggerated the impacts of inflation and distorted what we buy, but really, inflation wasn't a linear thing or a constant

---

[86] Helliwell, John F., Richard Layard, Jeffrey Sachs, and Jan-Emmanuel De Neve, eds. 2021. World Happiness Report 2021. New York: Sustainable Development Solutions Network.
[87] Per Desmond Henry, a Topeka, Kansas-based certified financial planner (CFP) https://www.forbes.com/advisor/retirement/top-10-retirement-tips-2021/

[89] https://www.pewresearch.org/social-trends/2020/12/09/how-the-coronavirus-out-break-has-and-hasnt-changed-the-way-americans-work/
[90] 90 https://www.couriermedia.com/product/courier-36 with additional detail https://go.451research.com/2020-mi-covid19-remote-work-influence-unified-com-munications-and-collaboration.html?utm_source=covidms

before COVID either. Microstrategy CEO Michael Saylor describes inflation is not a scalar function; it is a calculus that varies by item and location. Saylor details that the pandemic meant people did not buy many things; cruises, concert tickets, vacations and those prices fell. People rationally bought what they wanted and could buy -and so bonds and houses in the suburbs near large cities both hyper-inflated. Housing prices simultaneously decreased in many areas.[91]

Consumers appear to be spending less on food, but additional research is needed because the US Bureau of Labor and Statistics is having a difficult time collecting data to quantify the actual impacts of the pandemic on consumer expenditures.[92] BLS data for the Consumer Price Index, which measures the changes of prices of goods and services, is also citing changes in the methods of their reporting and less availability of data.[93] The trends over the past year are dramatic.

---

[91] Michael Saylor on YouTube https://www.youtube.com/watch?v=Vuz44fwkEz0
[92] https://www.bls.gov/covid19/effects-of-covid-19-pandemic-and-response-on-the-consumer-expenditure-surveys.htm
[93] BLS Consumer Price Index News Release September 2021 Table A https://www.bls.gov/news.release/archives/cpi_09142021.htm and www.bls.gov/covid19/effects-of-covid-19-pandemic-on-consumer-price-index.htm

%Change in Consumer Price Index for All Urban Consumers (CPI-U): U.S. city average[94]

Item			Unadjusted change in 12-months Aug. 2020 - Aug. 2021
All items			**5.3**
Food			**3.7**
		Food at home	3.0
		Food away from home	4.7
Energy			**25.0**
		Energy commodities	41.9
		Gasoline (all types)	42.7
		Fuel oil	33.2
Energy services			**8.6**
		Electricity	5.2
		Utility (piped) gas service	21.1
All items less food and energy			**4.0**
Commodities less food and energy commodities			**7.7**
		New vehicles	7.6
		Used cars and trucks	31.9
		Apparel	4.2
		Medical care Commodities	-2.5
Services less energy services			**2.7**
		Shelter	2.8
		Transportation services	4.6
		Medical care services...	1.0

Source: BLS Consumer Price Index News Release September 2021 Table A
(Note: City size is not normalized in this data.)

---

[94] BLS Consumer Price Index News Release September 2021 Table A
https://www.bls.gov/news.release/archives/cpi_09142021.htm

Unique to the US

I can't tell you what is important to you; I can just guide you with ideas to cull through and then give you lots of data about the places that might meet those criteria.

In researching all the data on what makes people happy in general, in partnerships, work, moving, retirement, getting older, I dove into over a few hundred research papers and books, diving down the rabbit hole to gather and distill it all. I'm hoping you benefit from my obsessive reading.

When I read the 2019 World Happiness Report; it was the most depressing thing I've read in ages. I write this not to ruin your day, but because it is a startling reminder of how maintaining/ensuring our own well-being is critical for ourselves, our loved ones, and society.

All of the stories I've heard about challenges due to COVID, retirement, work, divorce, health issues, frustration and discontent are more than personal sagas. They are part of a large trend, unique to the US, of growing unhappiness. Again per the 2019 World Happiness Report:

"The years since 2010 have not been good ones for happiness and well-being among Americans. Even as the United States economy improved after the end of the Great Recession in 2009, happiness among adults did not rebound to the higher levels of the 1990s, continuing a slow decline ongoing since at least 2000 in the General Social Survey.

By most accounts, Americans should be happier now than ever. The violent crime rate is low, as is the unemployment rate. Income per capita has steadily grown over the last few decades. This is the Easterlin paradox: As the standard of living improves, so should happiness – but it has not."[95]

Further, the report indicates Americans are declining in health, social trust and confidence in government. 49% of

---

[95] Helliwell, J., Layard, R., & Sachs, J. (2019). World Happiness Report 2019, New York: Sustainable Development Solutions Network.

Americans are addicted to one or more things at a given time (substances, gambling, excessive digital media, work, and sex were cited). Global and US data demonstrate that unhappier people seem to hold more populist and/or authoritarian attitudes.

Social scientist Carol Graham's book, "Happiness for All?" analyzes Gallup data and highlights trends in wealth inequality and its impacts on the US which translate into mental health inequality.

- The US has become less happy since the early 1970s.
- Mental well-being has become more unequal in the US
- America is suffering from a lack of hope. That is dangerous. Unhappy people do not invest for their own long-term well-being.
- Compared to the rich, those who are poor in the USA have higher levels of stress, pain, and lower life satisfaction.
- Life satisfaction is reduced by living in an area with high income inequality.
- Americans have lost confidence, and are correct to have done so, in their hopes of upward social mobility.
- The optimism advantage of blacks over whites in modern America is approximately twice that of the optimism advantage of rich people over poor people
- Americans in midlife have particular psychological difficulties.
- The happiness and financial-satisfaction levels of Americans with low amounts of education have fallen behind Americans who have large amounts of education. Well-being gaps of this sort have thus widened over the last five decades. In that sense, consistent with Carol Graham's thesis, psychological inequality has gone up in the United States of America.[96]

---

[96] Blanchflower, David G. and Oswald, Andrew J., Unhappiness and Pain in Modern America: A Review Essay, and Further Evidence, on Carol Graham's Happiness for All? IZA Discussion Paper No. 11184, Available at SSRN: https://ssrn.com/abstract=3081418

The 2019 World Happiness Report data supports these findings as well. While happiness increased during the latter portion of 2020 and into 2021[97], the long-term trends don't look good.

This makes choosing your happy place all the more urgent...so let's get to the cheat sheet of takeaways.

Photo on Unsplash by: Briana Tozour Labjn

[97] https://news.gallup.com/poll/351932/americans-life-ratings-reach-record-high.aspx

Cheat Sheet to Happiness

Part 1: What makes a happy place for anyone?

Summarizing the happiness findings to use in your plans:
The pivotal effects are:

1. **Having basic needs met**
2. **Social Connectedness**
3. **Working towards goals and achieving them**

Designing your life to include the essential social connections and your sense purpose is critical for happiness and longevity. Health and wealth are important too but not critical. Having this clarity can be helpful when planning out the necessary steps to thriving in your next stage of life.

Part 2: What makes it a happy place for YOU specifically?

CHOOSE MY HAPPY PLACE BLUEPRINT
Why do I want a change?
What fears or beliefs limit my thinking?
What makes people happy in general?
What makes me happy specifically?
What is my priorities short list?
What is my plan and next steps to take?
Are the new changes working well; how to improve?

Hint: The answer probably isn't in a Top 10 list from someone else; it's your own unique priorities: who and what's important to you.

Get Clear and Get there Sooner. The shortcut to your Happy Place

Many people spend more time planning a vacation than what they're going to do with their lives. The key question to ask yourself is: what are you looking forward to? Your unique priorities are the most important set of decisions you need to make to thrive.

4 - What specifically makes ME happy?

Let's Build Your Priorities Short List

WOO HOO! Now that you know why you want to change your life, how you can reign in and reframe fears, and know what makes people happy and the current trends, let's move to the fun part to build your Priority Short List -which is a picture of what you are looking for.

And don't forget, this is a quick first cut. You will want to come back to this. Answer these questions in iterations. On your first pass, just fill in "My Specific Criteria in this Category". The brain cannot come up with ideas and edit ideas concurrently, so you'll fill in the list, then you'll think about if you have this now or can adopt it here and now, before moving on to the Top 6 Picks.

Download the free companion workbook

To make this work easier to do, download the free Priorities Workbook here to fill in your answers.
https://www.choosemyhappyplace.com/priorities-workbook

Why

We talked about this early in the book, but if you haven't done written your Why yet, do it now. It's important. Answer the following questions for yourself:

- *Why do you want to move or change?*
- *What about this change will make your life better?*
- *What is missing in your life now?*
- *Extra credit: Take out a separate pad of paper and write a letter from your future self - Describe why you are so happy that you retired/moved/made this life change and what you absolutely love about this new life. Include lots of details!*

Who

Who do you want to be?

I'd also suggest considering who you admire, adore, envy, as all of those can illuminate unowned aspects of yourself you should develop.

First there is you yourself. What is your identity in this next stage of life? What do you enjoy and will you be able to do so in the places you're considering?

> **"Research suggests we're happier when we have many aspects to our identity"**
>
> - Gretchen Rubin

Who do you want to be near? How near (an hour away or next door?)

Jim Rohn says we are the average of the five people we spend the most time with, if that is true, who are you living near and spending time with in your ideal future self's life?

You love your loved ones: parents, children, grandchildren, but is where they live where you want to live? How likely is it that they will still live in the same place in 10 years?

Where to live might not be a decision you're making alone. This can be challenging; having more criteria may be a great way to compare competing priorities and negotiate a best fit. It can give you a more objective way to score.

There are friends and family you may want to be near, but you may not want to be next door to them. Who has brought you happiness in the past?

Community

Community are people who you'd enjoy being surrounded by. What makes you feel connected and how much connectedness you prefer is unique to you. Do you want a diversity of ages, races, interests in your community?

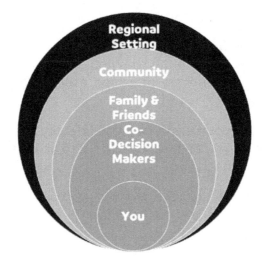

The regional setting influences who lives in an area. From urban or rural, the type of landscape and how people enjoy it, to culture – how good are the local coffee shops, museums, bookstores, restaurants makerspace, farmers markets, politics? Are there university classes and performances, can you see live music, or the ballet, hike a mountain, play tennis, go for a swim year-round? Is your favorite yoga nearby, or church, or a good local groups, or even your favorite foods? Is the library decent, is there good pho nearby?

On a regional scale, demographics become important to wellbeing and connections. The hospitals, the number of doctors per 100k of population, the vacant housing rates, and more.

Your neighbors also matter to your well-being.

If driving is not always feasible to stay connected - are there airports, senior services, public transportation, bike paths, Uber or Lyft or taxis? It will surprise many people that all of these options are not actually available everywhere in the US.

Find Your Tribe

Who is in your tribe? How close by are they? Who's currently important to you and who do you want to be around to be your best self?

Finding your tribe when you move somewhere new is essential. There are the obvious places: family, friends and friends of friends, churches, civic volunteer organizations, professional groups, parents of your children's friends, hiking clubs and social clubs. Plus, I love events from bookstores and libraries, maker spaces, REI or hiking clubs, local universities or anywhere with ongoing classes, art barns, historical societies and museums. All are wonderful!

There are also ways to meet people while trying something new, and so here are a few of my favorites for meeting in person:

1.   Atlas Obscura[98]: a wonderful travel site for going off the beaten path, local tours and events and just a general rabbit hole of curiosities to explore.

2.   Meet Up[99]: full of all kinds of classes, meet ups, and groups to gather. I have loved the Baltimore Agile group, 3d printing in MD, Malaysian cooking in DC, pitch fests, art events and openings, volleyball, and exploring new topics and meeting wonderful people as we learn together. The availability is uneven across the country, you can easily start an event of your own.

3.   EventBrite[100]: similar to Meetup but now with online events too- book clubs, to pickleball etc.

4. Creative Mornings[101]: a free monthly breakfast lecture series designed for creative communities, started by Tina Roth-Eisenberg.

---

[98] https://www.atlasobscura.com/
[99] https://www.meetup.com/
[100] https://www.eventbrite.com/
[101] https://creativemornings.com/

Are you in sync with loved ones' expectations? Who are you as a couple?

As you and your sweetheart do these exercises, I'd recommend doing them independently, and then comparing notes after.

Additional questions for couples from a recent retirement coaching article is a good start to uncover what your typical day might look like:

- "What is the honest assessment of the state of our relationship?
- What will our daily routine and our chores be when we're both at home?
- What is on my bucket list? What is on your bucket list? What is on our bucket list?
- What's our lifestyle going to look like?
- Are we going to have breakfast and lunch and dinner together?
- Will either of us work in retirement?
- Where will we live?
- How often will we travel?
- How often will we see family?".[102]

---

[102] https://www.investmentnews.com/how-retirement-coaching-can-add-value-to-your-practice-65761

What

What are your non-negotiable essentials or Must haves?
What are your Nice to haves?
What are your Must Not haves?
Outline your typical day. What do you do, in detail, and what do you feel? Do you still work and if so part time/full time/seasonally/self-employed, etc.

In his book *The Art of The Good Life 52 Surprising Shortcuts to Happiness, Wealth and Success*, Rolf Dobelli suggests looking at your typical day to see how 'different' it will really be.

If you hate winter in VT and decide to move to FL, but then keep working indoors in an office, commuting in traffic, and still living the majority of your life the same way, except now without friends nearby to visit, is your move to FL really going to make you happier?

If you are retiring to FL, or moving for a job that thrills you, and have loved ones nearby, then that is a completely different scenario. [103]

What makes you happy or puts you into a state of flow?

Flow is the wonderful feeling where you lose yourself and all sense of time. Will your new place allow you to do more of that?

What has brought you happiness in the past?

The past is often a reliable indicator of what makes your life better or worse.

Where

Where do you feel at home?
Where do you feel energized?
Where are you already thinking of moving (to live or work)?
What about those places you're already thinking about is appealing?

Are you someone who loves the mountains? The beach? Cities? A midcentury house in the woods, a horse farm in the sticks, big sky country, a condo with city lights?

Where within that place do you feel at home? At a church, a park, a museum, a maker space, the library, the hiking trails, the community pool, the gym, lake, beach, Kiwanis, or Creative Morning Events, and the list of possibilities goes on and on.

You don't have to limit it to just one type of place yet, but rule out what won't work for you so you can focus your search more easily.

---

[103] https://www.amazon.com/Art-Good-Life-Thinking-Business-ebook/dp/B072MFPSJH

Where you live has a large impact on your predicted longevity. There is data by census tract for predicted longevity based on age and community amenities that contribute to wellness[104].

When

When are you hoping to make a change?

Are there external constraints?

Are there looming things like retirement or health issues that suggest a change sooner rather than later would be better?

What's your date to move, retire, make a change, or are you making smaller scale changes iteratively?

Set a date, you can change it later, but choosing a date will help you better plan.

Are you desiring to make a change, or expecting to make a change? The answer has a big impact on the likelihood of actually moving. So, if it's really important to you then you'll need to up the ante.

[104]https://www.rwjf.org/en/library/interactives/whereyouliveaffectshow-longyoulive.html?cid=xtw_rwjf_unpd_ini:usaleep_dte:20210105_des:flagship

How

*How will you prioritize between criteria?
How will you avoid optimizing for one
thing at the expense of your overall well-
being?*

*How can you apply the Pareto (80/20)
rule to this and frame the 20% of your
essentials that will give you 80% of the
possible improvements?*

You have the Choose MY Happy Place process to follow which tells you may need to seek expert financial, insurance, real estate, medical, or other advice, as needed.

If you are planning a move, then GO VISIT! There will be things you didn't think of, can't quite articulate that make somewhere feel more like home. It might even be Multi-Sensory. Financial experts have told me: don't just visit once, do a pilot there; live for a year, and see if you like it before you buy a house. Getting priced out of your original market is not uncommon.

Expert Inputs

There are some key items to consult with your experts including:

Additional Tax data

For estate tax, business tax, capital gains and more by region see www.taxfoundation.org and consult with your financial advisors.

Financial advice particular to you

Of course, this influences where you might choose and the transition plan to move or change your life and should be handled by you and any financial advisors.

Medical facilities best for your health

While there is data for average cost and outcomes per common health condition, you and your medical team are best to determine whether location is critical for your wellbeing.

Fear of not finding a good doctor keeps many from moving far from where they live now. That is understandable. If you do really want to move somewhere new, what's the best way to find good new medical care? Tap your social network and then look into these resources:

Dr. Peter Attia has a wonderful post on the attributes to look for in a doctor, and the questions to ask to find a doctor who will be a good advocate, affable, and able to help. [105]

OpenMD[106] has a nice list of not just online patient reviews but also peer review sites and hospital ratings by governmental and private reviewers.

Consumer Checkbook [107] is an independent research arm of Consumer Reports for local markets. They use a similar approach but instead of product reviews local services such as doctors, roofers, plumbers, auto repair shops, etc. They are terrific, and while the ratings are only in a few areas, their Advice guides of what to look for and consider are really helpful in the Healthcare Providers section and beyond.

Real Estate

There are so many differences within a single place just by neighborhood. After you've discovered your short list of places, consult a local agent, talk to locals, talk to Airbnb hosts, and online services to see real estate particulars. And visiting. Many financial advisors recommend trying a new place for a few months or even a year before selling an existing house or

---

[105] https://peterattiamd.com/how-to-find-a-good-doctor/
[106] https://openmd.com/
[107] https://www.checkbook.org/

a final move. Livability.com has a nice summary of services and hotels that let you test living in a new place.[108]

Local Neighborhoods & Flavor
A single place can vary greatly by neighborhood. Friends, family, travel sites and Airbnb hosts and experiences are a wonderful way to have a sense of local area. Of course, visiting and assessing for yourself, as the ultimate expert. It is recommended to see shops, trails, amenities, services and flavor. There are some criteria that are not easily expressed or measured that only visiting will tap into. But advice from others may make the learning curve shorter.

Senior Services
Senior services available can be vastly different by region with rural areas having limited or sometimes no providers nearby. Service data is typically proprietary but very useful to see relative cost and availability by area. This resource is a good place to start:

https://www.aplaceformom.com/planning-and-advice/senior-housing-101/senior-housing-costs/senior-living-cost-planner

Insurance
Insurance rates are frequently changing, and based on credit ratings, storm and flood risks, and other very localized and personal data. This is a topic you should seek expert estimates for when comparing locations.

Per insurance.com for example, Average Renters Insurance Can Vary by 7x times! depending on which state you live in. https://www.insurance.com/home-and-renters-insurance/coverage/renters-insurance-guide.html

There are many tools and experts to determine your rates. Here is one example: https://www.insurance.com/home-and-renters-insurance/home-insurance-basics/5-factors-that-affect-rates.html

---

[108] https://livability.com/topics/make-your-move/the-ultimate-guide-to-test-driving-a-new-city-before-you-move-there

Home owners and renter's insurance can be prohibitively expensive or nonexistent if you live near the water or other risks.

Legal Advice
Before you move, and if you do move, reputable law firms are essential for estate plans or a business legal advice in both your current and the new locations.

5 - My Priority Short List

WOO HOO! Now for the fun part to pull all that into your Priority Short List -which is a picture of what you are looking to have in your life. Let's build this!

Any surprises in all those criteria? The insight that public radio is essential for public health was amazing to me! That most people choose where to live based on money alone, even though the costs do not vary that dramatically and that is not what makes people happy too.

Now let's cull that list, plus your What Makes Me Happy List (Who/What/Where/When/Why/How) to see your **Priority Short List**! And we are going to just fill in the specific criteria for now. IN a later chapter we will and mark off the criteria you have where you live now or could adopt now. The final pass will identify the top 6 or so priorities for your short list.

Look at this list and ponder:

- Do any places to move to or changes you're considering come to mind?
- Does anything come off the list?
- Do you have much of this now where you are living? Would you consider staying put?
- Can you add more of this to your life where you are living now whether you move or not?
- Does anywhere that you were considering moving to change in its rank based on meeting or not meeting your criteria?

Why
- Why do you want to make a change?
- What about this change will make your life better?
- What gaps are missing now?

▶ My Top 6 Picks
✓ Do I have this now?
☐ Could I adopt this now where I am or does it require a change?

Who

- Who do you want to be?
- Who do you want to near? How near?
- Who is your tribe or community?
- Who do I depend on for what?
- Who depends on me for what?
- Am I in sync with loved ones on expectations?

▶ My Top 6 Picks
✓ Do I have this now?
☐ Could I adopt this now where I am or does it require a change?

What

- What brings you joy or a state of flow?
- What's non-negotiable, essential, must haves?
- What are your Nice to haves?
- What are your Must Not haves?
- What do you want in your typical day?
- How much does your typical day differ in a new setting?
- What brought you happiness in the past?

▶   My Top 6 Picks
✓   Do I have this now?
☐   Could I adopt this now where I am or does it require a change?

Where

- Where do you feel at home?
- Where do you feel energized?
- Where are you already thinking of moving (to live or work)?
- What about those places you're already thinking about is appealing?

▶ My Top 6 Picks
✓ Do I have this now?
☐ Could I adopt this now where I am or does it require a change?

When

- When are you hoping to make a change?
- Are there external constraints?
- Are there looming issues that suggest a change sooner would be better or unavoidable?
- What's your date to move, retire, make a change, or are you making smaller scale changes iteratively?

▶ My Top 6 Picks
✓ Do I have this now?
☐ Could I adopt this now where I am or does it require a change?

How

- How will you prioritize between criteria?
- How will you avoid optimizing for one thing at the expense of your overall well-being?
- Can you apply 80/20 to this list?
- How will you prioritize between your criteria and your partner's criteria?
- Can you use Pick 6 in this process of how you pick?

▶ My Top 6 Picks
✓ Do I have this now?
☐ Could I adopt this now where I am or does it require a change?

Expert Inputs

Additional Tax Advice

Financial Advice particular to you

Medical facilities best for you

Real Estate & local neighborhoods

Senior Services

Insurance

Legal

▶   My Top 6 Picks
✓   Do I have this now?
☐   Could I adopt this now where I am or does it require a change?

Detailed Criteria/ Priorities

▶ **My Top 6 Picks**
✓ **Do I have this now?**
☐ **Could I adopt this now where I am or does it require a change?**

Weather & Climate Change

Setting, landscape, green space, activities available

Schools/University Town

Shopping

Indie- Independent radio, businesses, maker spaces, etc. available

Museums, Music, Arts, Culture

Hobbies & Leisure

▶ My Top 6 Picks
✓ Do I have this now?
☐ Could I adopt this now where I am or does it require a change?

Ancestry, education, race, religion or other local demographics

Average Income

Income Inequality

Cost of Living (Taxes of all flavors, Food, Medical, Transportation, etc.)

Housing & Architecture

Religion

Politics

Business climate (is this a good state to start a business?)

Crime

Job Opportunities

Commute & Transportation (Traffic, taxis, car services, mass transit)

    ▶   My Top 6 Picks
    ✓   Do I have this now?
    ☐   Could I adopt this now where I am or does it require a change?

Public Libraries

Local Medical Care Availability and Quality

Senior Services (Transportation, In-home Care, Physical Therapy)

Local Events

Walkability

Gyms, Athletic Facilities, Trails

Culture, Local Neighborhoods & flavor

Blue Zones, Social Capital, Happiness Level of a place

MY PRIORITY Other items:

▶ My Top 6 Picks
✓ Do I have this now?
☐ Could I adopt this now where I am or does it require a change?

WOW! What A List! It looks amazing! Congratulations!

Deciding on your short list
With this list, let's go back through and figure out the scores!

Score Potential Places Against Your Top Criteria: A formula to reduce overwhelm

In **Algorithms to Live By**, Daniel Kahneman says it's better to trust an algorithm than your own gut, and this is backed by volumes of research. His approach applied to a move:

- Pick crucial traits (limit it to six) that your ideal place will have
- List how you evaluate each criterion and how you will score it (e.g. Scale of 1-5 or 1-100).
- Score each place across these 6 criteria on the list, tally them up, and—no matter what—commit to visiting the candidate places with the highest final score.

Go back to you're the Prompts of Priorities and identify your top 6.

My own nomenclature is to use these symbols next to each criteria.

- ▶ **My Top 6 Picks**
- ✓ **Do I have this now?**
- ☐ **Could I adopt this now where I am or does it require a change?**

Download the free reports or join one of the upcoming Choose MY Happy Place Picking Places Bootcamp, and it includes Our Selection Tool with admission, to save you hundreds of hours of research with over 700 criteria for each of 382 US Places.

Focus on Now

If you're still unsure about a decision, author of **Personal Development for Smart People**, Steve Pavlina, has a wonderful suggestion for a quick gut check.

"If I were to commit to this choice, how would it affect me right now? What immediate changes would I experience?

Imagine each possible choice as real, as if you've already made it. Pay attention to how the choice makes you feel. Does it feel good, or does it feel wrong somehow?" [109]

---

[109] https://stevepavlina.com/blog/2008/12/overcoming-indecision/

Bloom

WHERE YOU ARE PLANTED

Bloom here & now?
With this list, let's go back through and figure out:

- Do you have much of this now where and how you are living now? Would you consider staying put?
- Can you add more of this to your life where you are living now whether you move or not?

Update the table and see- you might not need to move to be in a happier place.

Were you surprised looking at your Criteria Shortlist? Were there a lot of those items you could have here and now, to make your life better sooner? Or did it really amplify how much you'd like that is missing where you are? (and therefore, motivate you to move)

While the data does indicate people are happier after a move, it also shows the majority of you will choose to not move. So, then bloom where you're planted. I've seen that from people in my events too. Life hacks for being happier anywhere come straight from your Priority Short List.

"When it comes to relocating, "nothing you focus on will make as much difference as you think," wrote Schkade and Kahneman. This doesn't mean that you won't (or can't) be happier in a new place, but that increasing happiness in your living environment requires more than just a change of scenery. With that in mind, here are some of things that can actually lead to more satisfaction with where you live and that are worth looking for in a new home if you're on the hunt for a happiness boost" [110]

- Improving work/life balance: most especially with shorter commutes
- Increasing Social connection: People and quality of your community is one of the biggest indicators of happiness
- Improving your living environment: While cities offer lots of food and culture, countryside is idyllic, suburbs are where people are most happy.

"The secret to getting more out of your move: plan, and don't just move for the sake of moving. Try to pinpoint exactly what you're lacking in your current home, then look for a home that can improve on those specific factors."[111]

---

[110] https://www.moving.com/tips/can-moving-make-you-happier/
[111] https://www.moving.com/tips/can-moving-make-you-happier/

Timing

You may not need to wait, with the recent surge in remote working.[112]

80% of organizations have implemented or expanded universal work-from-home policies as a result of Covid-19,

67% expect those policies to remain in place long term or permanently.

451 Research & Courier Magazine Aug/Sept 2020

[112] https://www.couriermedia.com/product/courier-36 with additional detail https://go.451research.com/2020-mi-covid19-remote-work-influence-unified-communications-and-collaboration.html?utm_source=covidms

Look in your hands- You have a Priority Short List that gives a picture of what you are looking for in your happy place!

 *A star for you!*

We started this workbook with your Why. And you will want to come back to it, but to keep up your momentum and motivations you may also want to think about the whole enchilada, a few of them actually.

The first is the effect of happiness is improving your life, but that ripples out to the happiness of those around you.

Per the data, happier people: Are happier, healthier, live longer, spread happiness to others and make a community better.

Let's create happier lives. Let's choose our happy places.

A Few More Thought Frameworks & Tools

A few tools and concepts from engineering that I apply to life because I find them useful in planning and decision making.

Making time
Scheduling and regularly taking time to remind yourself of your why, and then plan your goals, rocks and tasks to improve your life is essential to making progress and it is iterative. An hour a week or every other week to check in, and see your progress towards plans, and make adjustments will do wonders to keep you moving forward.

If you want support to do this in a community of people moving towards thriving, join the Choose MY Happy Place Inner Circle where we'll have learning and working sessions to keep up your momentum.
https://www.choosemyhappyplace.com/blog

Gap analysis
Where do we want to go? Where are we now, how to close the gap? This makes plans very tactical and can be helpful to start making progress. Typically done in a spreadsheet.

Mind maps
I'm a big fan of spreadsheets and gap analyses, but you may not be. For some people, drawing out these ideas in a free-flowing mind map is easier to think about then rigid tables and spreadsheets; some prefer a letter from their future self. Use what works for you. Just draw your dream life.

Letters from your future self

Many authors talk about writing a letter from your future self to your current self as a way of imagining you are living your ideal life, and creating a better future now because of it. Author Sonja Lyubomirsky, in her book **The How of Happiness,** describes repeating this exercise daily for 4 or more days to better articulate that vision and start to see how to make progress more quickly. This is a new addition to my morning pages. Day dream for a few minutes about where you could be.

Pomodoro Sessions

Pomodoro sessions are brief timed work sessions, often done with others for accountability.

There are times you are feeling over tired and unmotivated. Sit down anyway and spend 20 minutes to just do whatever planning or task you need to do. You only have to do 20 minutes. Also called time boxing, this will help you overcome resistance. You might even call a friend to Zoom and each do this on your own tasks. I have often found that a group of us will sit down to this at 10pm, after work and be thinking we might not make it through 20 minutes. Then we are all surprised that we do all continue and do a few sessions because we are on a roll. But even if it's just 20 minutes, that can be so very powerful. And really it should be used for more than house cleaning most people use the method for.

In the wonderful Tim Ferriss interview of Jerry Seinfeld, Jerry Seinfeld says he tells his daughter "Sit and set a timer and create for an hour day and then stop. Enjoy the reward of stopping. You would never exercise without knowing how long, why would you do anything like that?" [113] Genius!

If you want support to do this in a community of people moving towards thriving, join the Choose MY Happy Place Inner Circle where we'll have learning and working sessions to keep up your momentum.
https://www.choosemyhappyplace.com/blog

---

[113] https://tim.blog/2020/12/09/jerry-seinfeld-transcript/

Ishikawa/Fishbone Diagrams

These diagrams are used for identifying root causes, asking 5 Whys along each branch to build a list of everything that can lead to an outcome. (either a good or bad outcome). For example: What can stop you from making your move or what could make your new hometown not ideal? It helps to frame and focus your thinking. I also find it really useful for depersonalizing challenging conversations within families by shifting the details to focus on what can contribute to a successful or unsuccessful move or action, rather than on disagreement. It can then be used to plan how best to move forward. Here is a sample Fishbone to give you a flavor of it.

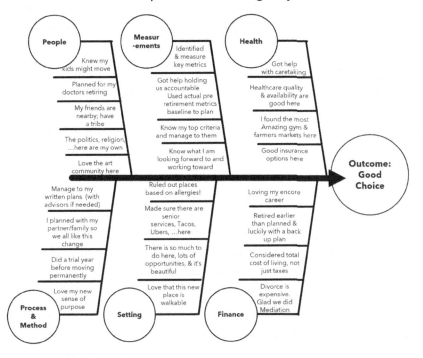

Cliff Hanging

"The best way is always to stop when you are going good and when you know what will happen next. If you do that every day when you are writing a novel you will never be stuck. That is the most valuable thing I can tell you so try to remember it"

-Earnest Hemingway

Earnest Hemingway's quote, in my experience, applies to more than writing. When you don't have time to finish a plan, stop work at a cliff hanger spot. Leave off, not when you've exhausted your ideas, rather stop when you have the next few pieces already in mind, so that you jump right in the next day without delay. Seems counter intuitive, doesn't it? I initially resisted this concept, thinking I want to finish everything while I am on a roll. That can be true, but more often I have found cliff hanging can keep me making consistent progress on a large task more easily.

Tests & iterations
Be agile. Test; so that you can be influenced by the data, not old beliefs. Simple hacks like walking to a grocery store- is a mile too far to walk for groceries each week? Try it. Even if you don't have a store a mile away, park a mile away from your store. A mile might seem really long if you've bought kitty litter or if the weather is bad but unnoticeable if you're walking with a friend.

Also, note what you do in a typical week and what you think you'd like to do. Add more of what you'd like to do and see if you enjoy it. I imagined having a short commute would give me the time to exercise in the morning. I'm sure for some people it does, for me it did not. It was a nice improvement, but I am a night owl who hates waking up early, and I just slept the extra half hour. Moving to a place with great trails, that I could walk to does motivate me to exercise consistently.

Start now to test, wherever you live. Adopt what you can now and you will learn along the way. Test, measure, refine. Keep tweaking your priorities, criteria, lifestyle to make your life better. Iterate as you learn new information, from research, visits, expert advice, or your own testing. Realize it may take a few iterations until you get it right.

Collaborations

There are two parts to collaborations that make them valuable. One is the accountability. Ever notice that you're less to skip a workout if you're meeting a friend to do it?

The other part is synergy. Great projects are often done in collaboration and community. Talking about ideas and working together often leads to something better.

Use a Pomodoro, or just share a drink and a chat. Or take one of the Choose MY Happy Place Saturday bootcamps to hear what others are trying.

Explore Limits/Voluntary Simplicity

There is a concept called Voluntary simplicity, like a vacation to a rustic cabin, or other activity to keep your sense of appreciation for what you have and what actually contributes to happiness.

Walk in the cold makes your house feel warmer when you come back. My sweetheart has us on a YouTube bender of videos by Nathaniel Drew. We started with his exploration of living the daily routine of Picasso [114], moved to the other artists, and on to I Ate For $1 A Day[115], which is a nice twist on a classic stoic idea of voluntary simplicity to counteract taking things for granted.

In Nathaniel Drew's video, he was spending an increasing amount on food and was not any happier and decided to try a week-long experiment and at the end of it, his appreciation of

---

[114] https://www.youtube.com/watch?v=gJ7CyM1Zrqc&t=243s
[115] https://www.youtube.com/watch?v=XesZtdl7cb0

food and life went way up. It's like a reset/recalibration on what's essential.

Terence Conran, in his book Easy Living, talks about how people find joy on vacation "Easy living is about providing the means to experience things directly, without the distancing intervention of technology or the burden of too many possessions....On vacation, we find that we can manage perfectly well without nine tenths of what our home contains"[116]

There is another clever idea of money dials from Ramit Sethi. He has an interview with Tim Ferriss that is helpful[117]. The basic idea is to imagine how you could be really frugal on what you don't care about and spend 10x what is important to you (within your budget). Test it out and see if you're happier. It helps just to be conscious of what you spend money on and align it to what makes you happier.

Morning Pages
Another item I am passionate about, comes from Julia Cameron in her book **The Artists' Way** . She recommends one write out 3 pages long hand. I have expanded on it, taking tips on loving yourself and expanding ideas from James Altucher in his Choose Yourself Blog, adding a sketch, and using it daily.

Morning pages are essential to for a good life, for me. If you are feeling overtired, too busy, burned out, pessimistic, in pain, or negative .....morning pages can pull you through to a better place pretty quickly right now and to a much better place over time. If you are feeling joy, optimism, gratitude, full of ideas, calm, centered, at peace, ...morning pages will amplify the positive emotions and help you to stay in that mindset most of the time.

I know you are likely busy. If you only have a minute, then just write 3 things down that you are grateful for. Or If really busy then just think of 3 things & write them later in the day. If you have more than a minute, wonderful, use what time you can

---

[116] Conran, Terence. Easy Living. Soma Books, 1999, page 12.
[117] https://www.youtube.com/watch?v=ACYXvR2dO68

allow. If you are really not busy, doing these for 15 minutes each morning will bring a nice cadence to your day.

What do I write about in my morning pages? Six themes:

1.   **DREAMS**   I start with any dreams I had last night that I remember? Write it out before you forget; dreams are elusive but often so insightful.

2.   **3 THINGS I'M GRATEFUL FOR**   Write three ideas at least; if you are struggling to think of 3 things, then try to write 50 to really shift your view.. On a bad day it might be - I am grateful that I am alive, I am writing, and this writing helps. On most days, everything will start to feel like a gift to appreciate.

3.   **WHAT DO I LOVE ABOUT MYSELF** This one was difficult to do initially. It does get easier. This practice will change how you view yourself. It will move you to more loving kindness for yourself and others. It helps interrupt the negative self-talk most people don't even realize they've been doing all day.

4.   **3 IDEAS** on a meaningful topic that I want to improve. These might be things like items to research, who you want to follow up on about a place you're interested in, business ideas, things to improve a specific project, questions for financial advisor, etc.

5.   **PRESSING ITEMS** If there is anything pressing on my mind such as: my to-do list, mental clutter, recent surprises, I notice I am feeling ….If there is anything challenging, try to find 3 things that might be good about it. This is the lighter version of cognitive reframing. It can also be noticing patterns in relationships.

6.   **SKETCH** I usually do a Sketch. Your morning pages may work better if you hand write them. With all our time online, hand writing taps into different parts of your brain. No one cares what it looks like; this process is for you and you only.

Doing a sketch puts you into a meditative state. It might make you laugh out loud. You will love coming back to it later. Even just a doodle will ignite more creativity and joy. Your day will be brighter because of it.

Carve at least a minute for gratitude as a small slice of autonomy in an overextended life. It will make your day better. If you can, expand to include a sketch, and maybe all 6 topics, it will be a joy in your life.

The more you do this, the easier it becomes. You will find this sense of gratitude becomes your new baseline. Writing morning pages brightens your future days too. You will surprise yourself with things you've forgotten. With how lucky you are. Look at this whole book of wonderful things in my life.

A life worth living is a life worth writing about. Write your morning pages to craft your life narrative to be one that you love.

Free Resources to help on Choose MY HAPPY PLACE.com:

I invite you to subscribe for reports on new tools and insights and to download the Free Resources including the Intro to Happiness, The Cost Report, Income Inequality Report, and Climate Report describing detailed data for 382 US locations by visiting: https://www.choosemyhappyplace.com/choose-my-happy-place-report-bundle

FREE
Resources

Planning, Iterating, Next Steps

If you want to join a community of people choosing their happy place with to support and ideas to help turn your dreams to reality, please join the *Choose MY Happy Place Inner Circle.*

We'll do working-sessions and learning sessions each month to help you get clear on what makes you happy, plan how to make things better, and keep iterating to keep moving forward.

⬇ **CLAIM MY INNER CIRCLE TRIAL**

https://www.choosemyhappyplace.com/blog

Acknowledgments

Heartfelt thanks to my wonderful generous tribe who've bounced ideas, collaborated, inspired, critiqued, and been early adopters, cheerleaders and a huge grace.

Most especially to Blythe McCarthy, Trudi Thun, Annaline Dinkelmann, Nancy Case, Bea Hawkins, Donna Arsenault, Denise Mallin, Susan Plano Faber, Karen Dredske, Alina Koos, Toni Marechaux, Sheryl Bedno, and Danielle Brigati.

Ryan Levesque, Allison Tugwell, Nikki Jensen & the Ask Method Team. Chandler Bolt, Rachael Williams, Ellaine Ursuy and the Self-Publishing School team. Seth Godin the AltMBA30 cohort (Team Orca) for reminding me how important writing and connection are to me. Thanks also to my husband Rick for breakfast picnics and tuna sandwiches to fuel the deadlines.

I appreciate your wisdom, kindness, expertise and inspiration.

Thank you to everyone who's joined the Choose MY Happy Place events and shared your stories and feedback -it makes this work a joy.

Thanks for joining me in this adventure, please share your story as you get to your happy place!

Author Bio

Rose Thun is the founder of Choose MY Happy Place, a website that provides the insights, tools, and push you need to imagine and reach the best place for you.

She's also a management consultant who helps build high functioning teams and bring projects to life. Her work as an agile advocate leading teams in software development and engineering across many industries and organizations, led to the insight that the happiness of a team and sense of purpose are the bedrock for success, however you choose to define it.

With Choose MY Happy Place, her focus shifts to applying those principles to personal well-being. In this book, she brings her quest to optimize and find joy to the challenge of choosing how and where to live so you can get to your happy place sooner.

Your Help Requested!

Thank You for Reading My Book!

Love this book?

Please don't forget to leave a review!

I really appreciate feedback and every review matters a lot!

I need your input to make the next version of this book, and future books better. And I want to start a movement of people choosing their happy places & happy lives.

Please leave me a helpful review on Amazon, or wherever you bought this book, or Good Reads, to let me know what you thought. It helps me, and it helps future readers.

I love seeing what you loved, what you could use more of, and how this helps you!

I appreciate it immensely.

Thanks So Much!

Best wishes,

Rose Thun

NOW IT'S YOUR TURN

To get the best experience with this book, you'll want to download and use the Choose MY Happy Place Priorities Workbook so you are able to implement faster and take the next steps needed to create your short list sooner.

While you're there, if you are feeling like you just want to see information about lots of US places, and not dive into your priorities yet, then get the **Free Reports Bundle** with lots of details that couldn't fit in this book.

Thanks so much for joining me on the Happy Place Choosing ride and I hope to see you in the *Choose MY Happy Place Inner Circle* to continue to support and feed ideas to help turn your dreams to reality. I'd love you to join us!

⬇ CLAIM MY INNER CIRCLE TRIAL

https://www.choosemyhappyplace.com/blog